A Trip to the Planetarium

by Becky Manfredini

 HOUGHTON MIFFLIN HARCOURT

PHOTOGRAPHY CREDITS: COVER ©Nancy Pierce/Photo Researchers, Inc.; 3 (c) ©Nancy Pierce/Photo Researchers, Inc.; 4 (t) ©sebikus/age fotostock; 5 (b) ©NASA; 6 (bc) Getty Images/Photodisc; 6 (br) ©Digital Vision/Getty Images; 7 (bl) ©Digital Vision/Getty Images; 7 (br) ©Digital Vision/Getty Images; 8 (bl) ©Gemini Observatory/Photo Researchers, Inc.; 8 (br) ©NASA Kennedy Space Center; 9 (bl) Lunar and Planetary Institute/NASA; 9 (br) ©HMH; 10 (b) ©Photodisc/Getty Images; 11 (t) ©Corbis; 12 (bl) ©Gerard Lodriguss/Photo Researchers, Inc./Getty Images

Printed in China

ISBN: 978-0-544-07298-5

12 13 14 15 0940 20 19 18 17

4500693652   A B C D E F G

Contents

Vocabulary

solar system

planet

Stretch Vocabulary

planetarium

asteroid

terrestrial planet

probe

gas giant

dwarf planet

constellation

Introduction

Welcome, everyone! Notice that we're seated in a circle in this auditorium. Now look up. Do you see a big, round roof? It's called a dome. A dome is a roof found in a planetarium. This is a building in which you will see and experience the solar system. The solar system is the sun and all of the objects in space that revolve, or travel around it. Look at the machine in the center of the room. It is also called a planetarium. It projects lights inside of the dome so you can see the changing positions and motions of the sun, moon, stars, and other objects in the universe. Now, sit back, relax, and enjoy the show!

In 1923, the first planetarium opened in Germany.

Earth rotates on its axis from west to east. Earth also revolves in a counterclockwise direction.

Sun, Earth, and Moon

Let's begin our space show with Earth, because it's our home! Earth is a planet, or a large, round body that revolves around the sun in a clear orbit, or path. The sun, a star that shines by its own light, gives Earth light and heat. It takes Earth about 365 days, or one year, to move in its orbit completely around the sun.

Earth moves in another way. Watch how Earth rotates, or turns on its axis. As Earth rotates in a counterclockwise direction, day changes to night. While half of Earth gets light from the sun, the other half is in darkness.

Now look at the moon. While Earth is revolving around the sun, the moon is revolving around Earth! It takes about one month for the moon to make one complete revolution around Earth. It takes about the same period of time for the moon to complete one rotation. That's why the same side of the moon always faces Earth.

Look at how the moon changes as it revolves around Earth. Phases are the changes in the appearance of the moon's shape as it orbits Earth. Did you know that the moon doesn't actually change shape? You are just seeing different amounts of the moon's lighted side as it revolves around Earth!

We see a full moon when Earth is between the moon and the sun.

Waxing Gibbous

First Quarter

Waxing Crescent

Full Moon

Moon's orbital path

Earth

New Moon

Solar radiation

Solar radiation

Waning Gibbous

Third Quarter

Waning Crescent

Terrestrial Planets

Now let's move on and look at the solar system's big picture! The solar system has eight planets. They are Mercury, Venus, Earth, Mars, Jupiter, Saturn, Uranus, and Neptune. Four of them are known as the inner planets and are the closest to the sun. They are Mercury, Venus, Earth, and Mars. They are also known as terrestrial planets because they are Earth-like. These four planets lie between the sun and the asteroid belt. This area between Mars and Jupiter has thousands of rocky objects.

After the sun formed, a cloud of rock, dust, and gas remained. These left-over materials formed the planets. The part of the cloud closest to the sun was the warmest. Rock and metal parts clumped together to form the terrestrial planets. They are small, rocky, warm, and dense.

Mercury is the smallest of the eight planets. Its orbit is closest to the sun.

Venus

Mercury

The terrestrial planets have a hard surface made of rock. Of the four inner planets, only Earth and Mars have moons.

The terrestrial planets revolve more quickly around the sun than the four outer planets do. Mercury, Venus, and Mars are closest to Earth, and have solid surfaces. Many space probes have been sent to collect information about these planets. Probes are spacecraft carrying scientific equipment to collect and record information.

These probes have collected images of volcanoes, large holes called craters, and deep cracks called faults. Some probes have landed on Mars and Venus. They have studied rocks and gases in the atmosphere.

Mars

Satellite images of Earth show large blue areas of water.

Mars is the fourth planet from the sun and is the most Earth-like of the terrestrial planets.

Earth

Gas Giants

Now look up and find the biggest planets in the solar system. The four outer planets are known as gas giants, because they are giant balls of gas! They are Jupiter, Saturn, Uranus, and Neptune. Jupiter is larger than all of the other seven planets combined. The gas giants are sometimes called Jovian, because they are Jupiter-like planets. *Jovian* is the adjective form of the word *Jupiter*.

The gas giants don't have solid surfaces like the terrestrial planets. Scientists think that inside each ball of gas is a very small, solid core. Compared to the inner planets, the outer planets are larger and less dense.

Jupiter is so large that more than 1,300 Earths could fit inside it!

Jupiter

Saturn

Each of the four outer planets has surrounding layers of gases, a ring system, and many moons. They rotate quickly, which makes for a short day. But the gas giants take a long time to revolve once around the sun.

Did you know that the gas giants are not all made of the same things? For example, Jupiter and Saturn are composed of liquid and gas that are mostly made of helium and hydrogen. Uranus and Neptune also have hydrogen and helium. But these two planets also have molten rock and melted ices.

A gas called methane makes up the atmosphere, or gas layer, that surrounds Uranus. High white clouds containing methane ice crystals blow across Neptune.

Uranus

Neptune is the farthest planet from the sun. You can't see it without using a telescope.

Methane gas gives Uranus its blue-green color.

Neptune

Dwarf Planets

Are dwarf planets similar to the other eight planets in the solar system? Yes! Dwarf planets are round or nearly round bodies that orbit the sun. They are like the other eight planets, but they're smaller. Some have strange orbits that cross orbits of other objects in the solar system.

The dwarf planets discovered so far are Pluto, Eris, Ceres, Makemake, and Haumea. In 1930, Pluto was discovered as the solar system's ninth planet. In 2006, the IAU (International Astronomical Union) changed its definition of the term *planet* and placed Pluto in the dwarf planet category. Objects that are smaller than the smallest planet, Mercury, are considered dwarf planets.

Before 2006, Pluto was considered the ninth planet and farthest away from the sun. Pluto is dark and cold because it gets very little sunlight.

Instruments, such as the Hubble Space Telescope, are used to observe Pluto and other faraway objects from Earth.

In 2008, the IAU named a new kind of dwarf planet, which scientists called a "plutoid." A plutoid is a dwarf planet whose orbit takes it farther from the sun than Neptune. Pluto, Eris, Makemake, and Haumea are dwarf planets that are plutoids. The dwarf planet Ceres is not a plutoid, because its orbit is much closer to the sun.

Constellations

Oooh! Ahhh! Look up at the night sky. Constellations fill the sky with their bright light. A constellation is a pattern of stars that forms an imaginary picture, or design, in the sky. As you know, a star is a hot ball of glowing gases that gives off energy. The word *constellation* comes from Latin words meaning "together" and "stars."

Ancient Greeks named many constellations. They chose names of people and animals from their myths, or stories.

As Earth rotates on its axis, constellations appear to move across the sky. They seem to rise in the east and set in the west. Above the North Pole, the constellations seem to move in a circle. When the seasons change, it seems as if the constellations change their position. This is because, as Earth revolves around the sun, we see different parts of space.

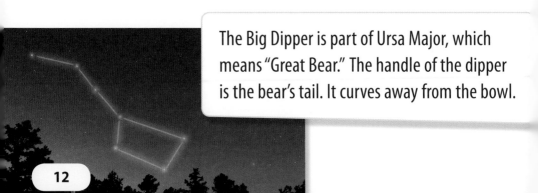

The Big Dipper is part of Ursa Major, which means "Great Bear." The handle of the dipper is the bear's tail. It curves away from the bowl.

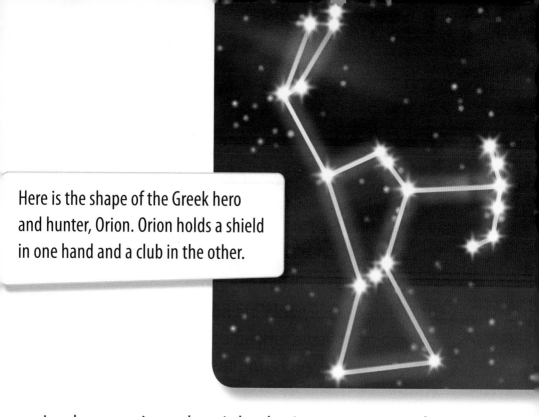

Here is the shape of the Greek hero and hunter, Orion. Orion holds a shield in one hand and a club in the other.

Look up again at the night sky. It may seem as if the stars in a constellation are close together, but they may not be. Some may be farther away than others. Astronomers find constellations very helpful. It's a way for them to find and identify the different stars in the sky.

Constellations change very little over time. It might take millions of years for a constellation to change its shape!

Model It!

Think about how Earth, the sun, and the moon move. Use the Internet or reference books to learn more about their movement. Then make models of Earth, the sun, and the moon. Work in a small group to show how all of the objects in the solar system move and work together.

Report On It!

Choose a terrestrial planet and a gas giant. Research how these planets are both similar and different. Draw a Venn diagram and record what you have learned about them on the diagram. Write a paragraph about each planet and draw pictures that show what they look like. Use your diagram and drawings to share what you learned with the class.

Glossary

asteroid [AS•tehr•oyd] Any of thousands of rocky objects that orbit the sun between Mars and Jupiter.

constellation [kahn•stuh•LAY•shuhn] A pattern of stars that form an imaginary picture or design in the sky.

dwarf planet [DWOHRF PLAN•it] A nearly round planet whose orbit crosses those of other bodies. Like the other eight planets but smaller.

gas giant [GAS JI•ent] An outer planet that is made of gas instead of solid matter.

planet [PLAN•it] A large, round body that revolves around a star in a clear orbit.

planetarium [plan•e•TAR•i•uhm] A machine that shows the changing appearances and positions of the sun, moon, planets, and stars. A building that houses the machine that projects lights on the inside of a dome to view the solar system.

probe [PROHB] A spacecraft carrying scientific devices to record and report information about objects in the solar system.

solar system [SOH•ler SIS•tuhm] The sun, the planets, and the planets' moons that move around the sun.

terrestrial planet [te•RES•tree•el PLAN•it] One of the inner, or Earth-like, planets in the solar system.